NIST CSF 2.0

Your essential introduction to managing
cybersecurity risks

NIST CSF 2.0

Your essential introduction to managing
cybersecurity risks

ANDREW PATTISON

IT Governance Publishing

IT Governance Publishing Ltd
Unit 3, Clive Court
Bartholomew's Walk
Cambridgeshire Business Park
Ely, Cambridgeshire
CB7 4EA
United Kingdom
www.itgovernancepublishing.co.uk

Formerly published in 2018 by IT Governance Publishing as *NIST Cybersecurity Framework – A pocket guide.*

This version first published in the United Kingdom in 2025 by IT Governance Publishing.

ISBN 978-1-78778-570-0

Cover image originally sourced from Vecteezy.

ABOUT THE AUTHOR

Andrew Pattison is the global head of GRC and PCI consultancy at GRC International Group. He has been working in information security, risk management and business continuity since the mid-1990s, helping large international organizations across many sectors. Andrew is a certified auditor, as well as holding CISM® and CRISC® certifications. He has provided extensive training in multiple GRC fields and is an approved APMG trainer.

ACKNOWLEDGEMENTS

I would like to thank Stuart Griffin, technical writer at GRC International Group, for his help with the development of this manuscript.

I would also like to thank Jonathan Todd, senior copy editor at GRC International Group, for his help reviewing the manuscript during the production process.

CONTENTS

INTRODUCTION

Cybersecurity is an ever-increasing concern for today's organizations. Customers, clients, and regulators expect their data to be protected and are quick to punish those they see as failing in this duty – a 2023 survey found that 66% of US customers would not trust an organization that allows their personal data to be breached, and 75% would stop buying from that organization.[1]

As a result, more and more organizations are choosing to implement a formal cybersecurity program (or formalize an existing, ad hoc program). Doing so not only safeguards information and systems but also the organization's reputation.

Origins of the CSF

In the years leading up to 2013, concern grew over increasing cyber threats to US critical infrastructure sectors. The growing use of IT and industrial control systems (ICSs) in these sectors, and the increasing degree of interconnectedness between these systems, opened the door to new cyber threats.

---

[1] Vercara, *Vercara Research: 75% of U.S.Consumers Would Stop Purchasing from a Brand if it Suffered a Cyber Incident*, December 2023, *https://vercara.com/news/vercara-research-75-of-u-s-consumers-would-stop-purchasing-from-a-brand-if-it-suffered-a-cyber-incident.*

Attacks on ICSs can result in significant harm to critical national infrastructure. The Stuxnet worm, detected in 2010, famously targeted Siemens control systems in Iranian uranium enrichment centrifuges and caused them to spin themselves apart.[2] Stuxnet was considered the world's first digital weapon, and has since been used as the basis for new worms: Duqu, Flame, and Gauss.[3]

In response to the rising number of threats, President Obama issued Executive Order 13636 (EO), "Improving Critical Infrastructure Cybersecurity," in February 2013. The executive order called for a voluntary, risk-based cybersecurity framework to be developed, outlining best practice for critical infrastructure sectors to manage their cybersecurity risks effectively. The result of this initiative was version 1.0 of the "Framework for Improving Critical Infrastructure Cybersecurity" (CSF), which was developed in collaboration with the cybersecurity industry, and published by the National Institute of Standards and Technology (NIST) in February 2014.

The first CSF was superseded by version 1.1 in April 2018, which was formalized and partly evolved on the basis of the Cybersecurity Enhancement Act of 2014 (CEA), passed in December 2014, calling for a *"prioritized, flexible,*

---

[2] M. Baezner and P. Robin, *CSS Cyber Defense Project Hotspot Analysis: Stuxnet*, Center for Security Studies, 2017, *https://www.researchgate.net/publication/323199431_Stuxnet*.

[3] Boldizsár Bencsáth, Gábor Pék, Levente Buttyán, and Márk Félegyházi, "The Cousins of Stuxnet: Duqu, Flame, and Gauss", *Future Internet*, November 2012, *www.mdpi.com/1999-5903/4/4/971/pdf*.

repeatable, performance-based, and cost-effective approach, including information security measures and controls that may be voluntarily adopted by owners and operators of critical infrastructure to help them identify, assess, and manage cyber risks."

In February 2024, version 1.1 of the CSF was superseded by version 2.0. This version sets aside the prior focus on industrial control systems and critical infrastructure in favor of a broader approach suitable for all types of organizations, reflecting the increasing popularity of the CSF among organizations in many different sectors inside and outside the US.

The NIST Cybersecurity Framework

The NIST CSF is designed to protect organizations from cyber attacks. Although it was originally developed to help US organizations involved in infrastructure systematically organize their cybersecurity activities and ensure they remain up to date, version 2.0 states that *"The CSF is designed to be used by organizations of all sizes and sectors, including industry, government, academia, and nonprofit organizations, regardless of the maturity level of their cybersecurity programs."*[4]

The framework is also not limited to US organizations: *"The CSF's taxonomy and referenced standards, guidelines, and practices are not country-specific, and previous versions of the CSF have been leveraged*

---

[4] NIST, *NIST Cybersecurity Framework version 2.0*, page 2, February 2024, *https://www.nist.gov/cyberframework*.

successfully by many governments and other organizations both inside and outside of the United States."[5]

Unlike many similar cybersecurity frameworks, the CSF does not specify the measures an organization should use to secure its systems or develop its cybersecurity program. Instead, it focuses on cybersecurity outcomes without specifying what must be done to achieve them, relying on cybersecurity risk assessment and a wide range of examples to derive appropriate and cost-effective controls that suit the business. This flexibility is a key reason for the CSF's ongoing popularity.

---

[5] NIST, *NIST Cybersecurity Framework version 2.0*, page 2, February 2024, *https://www.nist.gov/cyberframework*.

CHAPTER 1: AIMS OF THE FRAMEWORK

In its own words, NIST states in the preface to version 2.0:

"The Cybersecurity Framework (CSF) 2.0 is designed to help organizations of all sizes and sectors – including industry, government, academia, and nonprofit – to manage and reduce their cybersecurity risks. It is useful regardless of the maturity level and technical sophistication of an organization's cybersecurity programs. Nevertheless, the CSF does not embrace a one-size-fits-all approach. Each organization has both common and unique risks, as well as varying risk appetites and tolerances, specific missions, and objectives to achieve those missions. By necessity, the way organizations implement the CSF will vary." [6]

In short, the CSF is a voluntary framework, providing guidance for organizations to help manage their cybersecurity risks. This guidance is based on existing best-practice standards and guidelines, and provides a way of making other frameworks and control sets align with each organization's unique cybersecurity needs.

To understand how to secure your information, you first need to know what 'security' really entails. From a crude perspective, you might say that you want to stop criminals accessing your information. This is a laudable goal, but

---

[6] NIST, *NIST Cybersecurity Framework version 2.0*, page iv, February 2024, *https://www.nist.gov/cyberframework*.

only a fraction of what security is about. Information needs to be protected on three fronts:

- **Confidentiality:** Information should only be accessible to those who need access to it.
- **Integrity:** Information should be protected from unauthorized modification, destruction, and loss.
- **Availability:** The information should be accessible to authorized persons as and when necessary.

Information is, after all, only useful if it is correct and accessible to authorized persons. Protecting confidentiality alone does not constitute security – all three components must be addressed.

Relevant factors and variables

The factors that lead an organization to implement cybersecurity defenses and procedures will naturally vary depending on the organization's size, sector, business needs, and objectives. Such business objectives might be to meet the minimum standards for contract bids, which are likely to be made very clear by the contracting organizations, or to reach a defined level of maturity. The objectives could also be inspired by past disruptions that had an impact on productivity, in which case it is likely that there are clear metrics to aim for.

In addition to these, each organization will need to identify the types of threats and typical vulnerabilities it faces and the level of risk it is prepared to tolerate. An organization that relies on old, unsupported software and systems, for instance, will have very different needs than an organization that operates largely in the Cloud.

Implementation benefits

The CSF can be used to establish an entirely new cybersecurity program, to improve an existing one, or simply as an opportunity to review the organization's cybersecurity practices. By implementing the framework in accordance with their own specific circumstances, organizations can manage their cybersecurity risks in the most cost-effective way possible, maximizing the return on investment. As the CSF incorporates response and recovery, the organization also benefits from being able to quickly return to business as usual, while minimizing the risk of an incident in the first place.

The CSF also provides a 'common language' to aid cybersecurity communication both within the organization and with external partners. Using such a common language naturally helps limit confusion as to what is meant in contracts and other second- or third-party agreements. Meeting higher minimum standards increases opportunities for the organization to acquire new contracts and operate in other jurisdictions, as good cybersecurity practice tends to align with legal requirements that are increasingly common around the world.

The benefits of a common language also extend to communicating cybersecurity requirements to stakeholders, ensuring they are made aware of any risks to the organization. This clarity increases the likelihood that investments necessary to reduce or mitigate those risks will be provided, boosts awareness throughout the organization, and gains customers' trust by letting them know that you are protecting their data, in addition to their access to infrastructure and essential services.

Being able to effectively communicate with external partners will also help you keep up to date with constantly evolving cybersecurity threats and technologies – particularly those that are relevant to your industry or sector. While being aware of what is going on in your industry is always sensible, it also gives your organization the opportunity to improve existing defenses or implement new ones, based on any information you may receive from partners.

As the CSF draws upon various best-practice guidelines, your organization may already have a good chunk of NIST's recommended controls in place. However, your organization may also want to secure itself and have a structure in place to meet any later requirements. Such an approach would strengthen your existing measures, recommend guidance for areas of weakness, and let you implement any additional measures that may be necessary. Furthermore, identifying the organization's current practices first avoids unnecessary, duplicated work.

Structure

The framework has a relatively simple structure with three key components:

- **Core:** The core defines a broad set of cybersecurity outcomes that, taken together, comprise an effective cybersecurity program.
- **Profiles:** Profiles are used to map an organization's current and target cybersecurity status.
- **Implementation tiers:** Tiers can be used alongside profiles to categorize the maturity of a given measure

or outcome, with Tier 1 representing the least effective and Tier 4 the most.

The following chapters will explain each component in more detail.

CHAPTER 2: FRAMEWORK CORE

The framework core ('core') defines the high-level cybersecurity functions that protect your organization. It takes a structured approach to managing cybersecurity risk and outlines the key outcomes of implementing the framework. The core has three elements:

1. **Functions**
2. **Categories**
3. **Subcategories**

Figure 1 illustrates the core structure.[7]

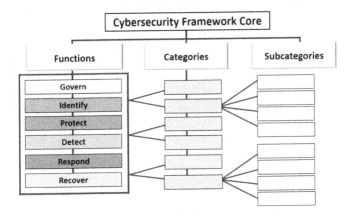

Figure 1: Framework Core Structure

---

[7] NIST, *NIST Cybersecurity Framework version 2.0*, page 3, February 2024, *https://www.nist.gov/cyberframework*.

Functions

The core contains six functions that outline key cybersecurity outcomes:

1. **Govern:** Understand the context in which the organization operates. Define policies, roles and responsibilities, risk management strategies, and oversight mechanisms, and manage cybersecurity risk in the supply chain.

2. **Identify:** Manage assets, identify and assess cybersecurity risks, and develop a continual improvement program.

3. **Protect:** Apply access, data, infrastructure, people, and platform controls to mitigate cybersecurity risks.

4. **Detect:** Monitor and analyze adverse events to determine if a cybersecurity incident has occurred.

5. **Respond:** Manage, analyze, and mitigate incidents. Manage incident reporting and communications.

6. **Recover:** Execute recovery plans and communications.

This approach to cybersecurity is broader than some other frameworks and includes processes that might ordinarily be considered part of a larger set of practices generally referred to as 'cyber resilience.' Cyber resilience combines cybersecurity or information security with business continuity, ensuring the organization not only minimizes the likelihood and impact of cyber attacks and other incidents but also improves how it responds to and ultimately recovers from those incidents.

Appendix A of the CSF lists all functions, categories, and subcategories. For ease of reference, each function, category, and subcategory is assigned a unique identifier. For example, under the Govern function, all the subcategories in the Organizational Context category are labeled GV.OC-XX. 'XX' refers to the sequential number assigned to the subcategory, so the fifth subcategory in GV.OC would be GV.OC-05.

Categories

Each function comprises multiple categories. These describe high-level outcomes that contribute to the associated function. For example, the Detect function comprises two categories: Continuous Monitoring and Adverse Event Analysis. Taken together, these two categories provide a solid foundation for detecting cybersecurity attacks and related incidents.

Subcategories

Subcategories are subdivisions of categories that describe more specific outcomes – whether technical or organizational – required to fulfill each category. For example, the Govern function contains six categories, one of which is Policy. Under the Policy category, there are two subcategories:

- *"GV.PO-01: Policy for managing cybersecurity risks is established based on organizational context, cybersecurity strategy, and priorities and is communicated and enforced."*

- *"GV.PO-02: Policy for managing cybersecurity risks is reviewed, updated, communicated, and enforced to reflect changes in requirements, threats, technology, and organizational mission."*[8]

It is up to the organization how to achieve these outcomes. For those needing help to get started, NIST's implementation examples (discussed later in this book) can be used to guide selection of appropriate actions and controls.

Framework profiles

Framework profiles ('profiles') describe how cybersecurity is handled within the organization, either currently ('current profile') or as an aspiration ('target profile'), in terms of the outcomes provided by the CSF. In essence, the profiles are a way for an organization to determine where its cybersecurity activities are now, and where they need to be. If an organization is particularly large or complex, it might develop multiple profiles, each aligned to a different component or business function.

Profiles do not necessarily need to encompass every outcome in the CSF. If your implementation is limited to a specific business function, for example, then some outcomes may not be applicable. Similarly, if your organization does not develop software, then outcomes related to secure software development would not apply. However, bear in mind that any exclusion should be backed

---

[8] NIST, *NIST Cybersecurity Framework version 2.0*, page 17, February 2024, *https://www.nist.gov/cyberframework*.

by a clear rationale so that you can explain its absence to stakeholders, clients, or other interested parties familiar with the CSF core.

You can also add outcomes relevant to your organization that the CSF does not include by default. For example, the CSF does not directly address privacy risks, despite most organizations holding some form of personal data (customers, employees). There is significant overlap between information security controls and privacy controls, but fully accounting for risks associated with privacy and personal data may require extra outcomes and controls to achieve them.

Current profile

The current profile is a picture of an organization's current cybersecurity activities expressed in terms of the outcomes in the CSF, and should be developed using a self-examination and assessment process. It is an opportunity for an organization to clearly establish its current level of cybersecurity readiness.

A current profile captures the cybersecurity measures already taken (which include any implemented controls, processes, personnel, etc.) and links them to the outcomes of the CSF. It then considers how these existing measures align with organizational and sector goals, regulatory and contractual requirements, and industry best practices, in addition to whether they reflect established priorities.

Target profile

The target profile describes the organization's intended destination for cybersecurity risk management activities, again expressed in terms of the CSF's outcomes. Target profiles are strongly tied to the organization's legal and regulatory requirements, contractual obligations, and business objectives.

Such objectives might be to meet minimum standards for a series of contract bids, which will probably have very clear cybersecurity objectives, or to reach a defined level of maturity, which might not have immediately apparent objectives. It could also be based on trying to improve productivity because cyber attacks have caused disruptions in the past, in which case there will be metrics that the target profile can aim for.

Other factors that have presumably already influenced the current profile, and should therefore also influence the target profile, are the organization's risk appetite and resources. Some of these factors, particularly resources, may act more like constraints than guidance. As such, in some cases the target profile may need to be adjusted to achieve organizational goals without being fanciful.

How the two profiles interact

After establishing the target profile, you can compare it to the current profile. This comparison should be used to prioritize actions necessary to achieve the intended outcomes and to estimate the overall cost and time commitment. This can also be used as a way of measuring the progress that has been made on the way to the target profile.

Ultimately, comparing the current and target profiles should show what still needs to be done to meet the organization's cybersecurity objectives. An action plan should then be developed to systematically address any gaps discovered and prioritize them accordingly. This might be based on risk, or on the basis that some are 'quick wins' compared to others that have complex dependencies. The action plan could even be phased, although at that point it may be advisable to develop several target profiles and move forward one profile at a time.

The two profiles can also be useful for top management before and during implementation, as they can be drawn up and presented to them – which is likely a necessary step to get them to commit to the project and view achieving the target profile as a business objective. Having clear senior management and/or board commitment to any project will also have a positive effect on the rest of the organization, reducing the chances that staff view the implementation process merely as a box-ticking exercise.

The most straightforward way of starting to develop the profiles is to identify how the organization relates to the framework core. Then, the established functions, categories, and subcategories can be aligned to the organization's requirements, risk tolerance, and resources. Ultimately, the profile is simply a record of the framework core as it applies to your organization – one outlining the current situation, and the other the intended goal.

NIST provides a template on the main CSF website to help organizations develop their profiles.[9] Additionally, some sectoral and industry bodies have developed community profiles for specific use cases. The Cloud Security Alliance,

---

[9] *https://www.nist.gov/cyberframework/profiles.*

for example, has developed a community profile for Cloud services. These community profiles can be used 'as is' or modified by the organization to suit its own needs.

Beyond this, the organization may wish to include additional information within its profiles, such as the location of implementation documents, the overall implementation status, board and/or management approval, and so on.

The profiles should be regularly reviewed as part of the continual improvement cycle in the CSF's Governance function. These reviews can be built into the implementation process at both the project and board level.

Target profiles may change as the organization's objectives and requirements change. New business opportunities, legislation, contracts, or the emergence of new threats or vulnerabilities could all require changes to a target profile.

Framework implementation tiers

Framework implementation tiers ('tiers') describe different degrees of sophistication that an organization's cybersecurity measures might have – specifically on the basis of its risk management process, integrated risk management program, and external participation. The four tiers are:

1. **Partial**
2. **Risk-informed**
3. **Repeatable**
4. **Adaptive**

The tiers are designed to describe how mature an organization's risk management processes are. As the risk management processes determine how cybersecurity risks are dealt with, the tiers naturally extend to describing the rigor of the organization's cybersecurity measures. They also give an organization some idea of the characteristics of risk management at increasing levels of maturity.

How to view the tiers

That said, the organization's current tier is not immediately correlated with the success of implementation – it merely describes the state to which the implementation is achieved. For instance, if your organization has only Tier 1 processes, implying that those processes have more than a few flaws, they can nonetheless be successful, assuming that the first tier was adequate for your organization's purposes.

As section 3.2 of the CSF specifies, *"Progression to higher Tiers is encouraged when risks or mandates are greater or when a cost-benefit analysis indicates a feasible and cost-effective reduction of negative cybersecurity risks."*[10] The 'correct' tier will enable you to meet your requirements, including business objectives and compliance obligations, without placing undue burden on the organization. However, reaching higher tiers will often mean that more business opportunities will be available to you, as you meet the criteria of more contracts.

---

[10] NIST, *The NIST Cybersecurity Framework version 2.0*, p.8, February 2024, *https://www.nist.gov/cyberframework*.

Each tier can be expressed in terms of either cybersecurity risk governance (corresponding to the Govern function) or cybersecurity risk management (all other functions). If the scope of your CSF implementation was limited to the Respond and Recover functions, for example, then you would only use the cybersecurity risk management components.

Generally, tiers are more effective when applied at the function or category level than to individual subcategories. The wording used in each tier reflects a broad picture of effectiveness that is not easily applied at the level of individual processes, policies, or controls.

Full descriptions of each tier are provided in Annex B of CSF version 2.0.

Tier 1: Partial

In the lowest tier, there are no structured or formal approaches to managing cybersecurity risks. Rather, risk is managed in a reactive, case-by-case manner. Assets are not mapped or managed and there is limited or no awareness of cybersecurity risk.

There are few or no processes to share cybersecurity information across the organization and there is no awareness of supply chain cybersecurity risk.

Tier 2: Risk-informed

At the second tier, cybersecurity risk management practices are established at management level, but not organization wide. Cybersecurity is considered in some areas of the business, but not all.

Risk assessments are performed but only in a subset of business operations. The process used is not repeatable, and there is no follow-up to ensure effectiveness or reassessment when the risk landscape changes. Cybersecurity information is shared, but on an informal basis.

Unlike the previous tier, at Tier 2 the organization is aware of its role in the larger ecosystem and the existence of risk within the supply chain, but it lacks a consistent or formal approach to mitigating supply chain risks.

Tier 3: Repeatable

Cybersecurity risks are now managed with consistent methods, which are documented in formal processes and policies throughout the organization. These are regularly updated based on changes in the organization's requirements or risk objectives, and changes in threats or technologies.

Staff are not just aware of their cybersecurity roles and responsibilities and have enough resources to fulfill them – they also have adequate knowledge and skills to perform them to defined standards. Those standards are updated as the organization's knowledge of risk evolves and in line with changes in the risk landscape.

Assets are monitored and there is regular communication at the executive level on current cybersecurity risks. The cybersecurity risk strategy accounts for risks arising from the supply chain, and there is a formal process to act on those risks and monitor the results.

Tier 4: Adaptive

In the highest tier, cybersecurity risk management practices are based on formal, rigorous processes and are informed by past experiences and predictive indicators. These processes are continually improved, allowing the organization to adapt its processes and policies as threats and technologies evolve, and requirements and/or risk objectives change.

The organization has a culture of strong cybersecurity awareness. Cybersecurity risks are considered no less important than financial or operational risks and are monitored by the executive team.

Real-time or near real-time monitoring is applied to ensure supply chain risks are quickly identified and acted upon, and cybersecurity information is shared across the whole organization and with relevant third parties.

How the tiers, profiles, and core interact

Ultimately, the three main points of the framework – tiers, profiles, and core – are closely connected. If your organization decides that it wants to implement the CSF to some degree, it can determine its current profile, which in turn helps identify its current tier. Both are informed by a variety of business needs, obligations, and objectives.

Based on its needs, the organization decides what its target profile will be. This equally informs the organization's needs for risk management and its corresponding tier. By comparing the current and target profiles, the organization can develop an action plan to progress toward its target profile. A crucial element of this will be developing the necessary risk management practices.

CHAPTER 3: CSF IMPLEMENTATION RESOURCES

Version 2.0 of the CSF is supported by a range of online resources designed to help users understand and implement the framework. These are available at the NIST CSF website.[11]

Informative references

Informative references map the outcomes of the CSF subcategories to guidance and best practices in other standards, frameworks, guidelines, and similar publications. They are intended to provide additional guidance on a given subcategory by highlighting how other frameworks and standards achieve the related outcome.

References associated with a given subcategory are not exhaustive, and more than one reference may be needed to fully achieve the relevant outcome. If you are unsure how to achieve the outcomes of a particular subcategory, these references should be your first port of call.

Informative references are not included in the CSF itself. They are available on the NIST CSF website through two methods: a downloadable spreadsheet and a web interface.

The spreadsheet – the NIST CSF 2.0 Reference Tool – is available under the 'Informative References (Mappings)' header on the website and contains all functions,

---

[11] *https://www.nist.gov/cyberframework*.

categories, subcategories, informative references, and implementation examples. The web interface provides the same information as the spreadsheet and includes search and filtering functions. For new users, the spreadsheet is probably easier to use.

NIST SP 800-53

One reference you will encounter frequently is NIST SP 800-53, *Security and Privacy Controls for Information Systems and Organizations.*[12] This document describes a large set of security and privacy controls intended for federal information systems and organizations. It is available at no cost from the NIST website.

It contains 20 families of controls covering topics such as access control, configuration management, media protection, and system and service acquisition. These controls are every bit as useful to commercial organizations as they are to federal ones, and anyone planning to implement the CSF should obtain a (free) copy to refer to during the project.

Implementation examples

Implementation examples are exactly what they sound like – examples you can use to help implement a specific subcategory. For example, in the Govern category, GV.OC-05 asks the organization to understand and communicate

---

[12] NIST, NIST SP 800-53 *Security and Privacy Controls for Information Systems and Organizations Rev. 5*, September 2020, https://csrc.nist.gov/pubs/sp/800/53/r5/upd1/final.

the outcomes, capabilities, and services that it depends on. It has two examples:

- *"Create an inventory of dependencies on external resources and their relationships to the organization's assets and functions."*
- *"Identify and document external dependencies that are potential points of failure and share them with relevant personnel."*[13]

Either option would likely be sufficient to achieve the intended outcome. However, the intent of the Govern category is to help the organization understand the circumstances in which it operates to allow more informed risk management decisions, so implementing both examples would be more effective than either one alone.

This is not to say that you must implement every example the CSF provides. How you achieve a given outcome should be derived from your risk assessment – if that indicates that you need a different approach from the examples provided, then you should develop a different way of achieving the outcome that suits your organization. Examples provide a useful starting point for development of controls and can help an organization increase the tier level associated with its chosen outcomes, but they are suggestions based on best practices, not requirements.

---

[13] NIST, *NIST Cybersecurity Framework version 2.0*, page 16, February 2024, *https://www.nist.gov/cyberframework*.

Quick-start guides

To help organizations get started with the CSF, NIST provides several quick-start guides on its website. At the time of writing, these guides cover:

- Developing profiles
- Developing community profiles
- Enterprise risk management
- Cybersecurity supply chain risk management
- Tiers
- Small businesses

These guides are a useful resource for organizations looking to implement the CSF. They offer varying levels of detail, so organizations will likely find some more helpful than others. Of particular interest should be the guides on developing profiles, enterprise risk management, and cybersecurity supply chain risk management, as these are critical to successfully implementing the CSF.

CHAPTER 4: CATEGORIES IN DETAIL

Govern

Previously a category under the Identify function, Govern is now a function in its own right. As a function, Govern is focused on identifying and understanding the regulatory and contractual requirements, dependencies, and other factors that the organization must account for when implementing a cybersecurity program, and on developing the policies, oversight, and governance structure needed to maintain that program effectively.

Organizational Context

Organizational context is about understanding the organization's objectives and operations, and the external and internal factors that affect how it operates. Its first subcategory is to understand the organization's mission and ensure it informs cybersecurity risk management – essentially, this means making sure that the cybersecurity program is proportionate to the size and operations of the organization.

This is followed by subcategories on understanding stakeholders and their requirements in respect of cybersecurity, and on identifying and managing cybersecurity legal and regulatory requirements (including obligations related to privacy and civil liberties). All organizations need to know what regulations apply so they can comply with the law, and they also need to know what degree of cybersecurity their stakeholders expect to be able to meet their expectations. In both cases, formal processes should be developed to track and manage legislative and contractual requirements, including periodic reviews to ensure legislative changes are accounted for.

The next subcategory asks the organization to understand and communicate critical objectives, capabilities, or services that external stakeholders expect or depend on. This helps the organization identify areas of higher risk and lays the groundwork for developing incident recovery plans.

Organizational Context's final subcategory asks the organization to understand and communicate the outcomes, capabilities, and services that the *organization* depends on. Like the previous subcategory, this feeds into development of incident recovery plans by highlighting systems that the organization needs to maintain operations.

Risk Management Strategy

This category is focused on laying the foundations for successful risk management. The first two subcategories ask the organization to establish risk management objectives and statements of risk appetite and risk tolerance.

Risk appetite or tolerance refers to the amount of risk an organization is willing to accept in relation to a given risk. It plays a key role in the risk assessment process by providing a baseline against which risks can be judged: Anything that exceeds the organization's risk tolerance must be mitigated to bring it within tolerance. Risk management objectives are broad overall goals for the risk management system, such as assessing 95% of risks within four weeks from the date they were identified.

The next subcategories require cybersecurity risk management activities and outcomes to be included in enterprise risk management processes, and a strategic direction that defines appropriate risk response options to be established and communicated.

The former addresses a common pitfall: All too often, cybersecurity risk is viewed as something separate from organizational risk and treated accordingly (often using separate processes with their own risk tolerance and methodologies). This approach fails to recognize that in the modern age of Internet-connected businesses, cybersecurity risk *is* organizational risk. Incorporating cybersecurity risk management activities into the broader enterprise risk management process improves visibility of all risks and lets the organization take a more consistent, holistic approach to risk management.

Similarly, defining a clear strategic direction and acceptable risk response options, and making sure that personnel are informed about them, also contributes to the wider business' understanding of, and effectiveness at, risk management.

The last three subcategories require that cybersecurity risks are communicated across the organization, that strategic opportunities are characterized and included as part of organizational discussions on cybersecurity risk, and that a standardized method for conducting cybersecurity risk assessments is established.

Communication around cybersecurity risks should be carried out across all levels of the business. It is particularly important that senior management and the board are aware and informed of the current cybersecurity risks facing the organization, as they drive the decisions that ultimately govern the effectiveness of the cybersecurity program. Inter-department communication and reporting should also be formalized, ensuring that everyone knows what to do if an incident occurs and that key risk decisions are acted on.

'Strategic opportunities' are also referred to as 'positive risks.' While most of the focus in risk management is on mitigating risks with a negative impact, some risks may also have a positive impact. Understanding and highlighting these opportunities during broader risk management discussions can benefit the organization.

Having a standardized cybersecurity risk assessment method is essential for effective risk management. The choice of method is up to the organization, but it should align with the defined risk tolerance and enable the organization to document, assess, and categorize cybersecurity risks in a consistent, repeatable manner.

Roles, Responsibilities and Authorities

Containing only four subcategories, this category is intended to ensure that cybersecurity roles and responsibilities are properly established and communicated. This category should drive accountability and improvement at all stages of the cybersecurity program.

The first subcategory asks that the organization's leadership foster an ethical, risk-aware, and continually improving business culture, and that they take responsibility and accountability for cybersecurity risk. Senior leaders must engage with and oversee both the implementation project and the long-term maintenance of the cybersecurity system. This doesn't mean that every senior leader should be a cybersecurity expert, but they should understand key concepts and the scale and nature of the cybersecurity risks faced by the organization. They should also encourage ethical practices and risk awareness across all business functions.

The second and third subcategories require that cybersecurity roles, responsibilities, and authorities are defined and that adequate resources are provided, in line with the cybersecurity risk strategy and the risks faced by the organization. Clear roles and responsibilities are a key part of any successful project, and many cybersecurity programs have failed because of under-resourcing.

The final subcategory requires cybersecurity to be included in human resources practices. This could include background checks for prospective employees or making cybersecurity training and awareness part of standard induction processes.

Policy

Although one of the most important components of any cybersecurity program, Policy only has two subcategories. The first asks the organization to establish a cybersecurity policy based on the context of the organization (discussed earlier as part of the Govern function), the cybersecurity strategy, and other relevant priorities, and to communicate and enforce the policy.

The details of this policy are up to the organization, but it should clearly define management's expectations in respect of cybersecurity and be signed off by senior management. The policy should be communicated across the organization, with employees required to acknowledge it on joining, and after any changes.

The second subcategory asks that the organization review and update the policy to reflect relevant changes (technological, regulatory, operational, etc.). Formal responsibility for conducting the review should be assigned to ensure that reviews are carried out, and the review frequency defined in line with the organization's risk tolerance. It can also be useful to broadly define the type and scale of changes that should trigger a review – for example, a corporate acquisition or other major organizational change, or a notable change in relevant technologies.

Oversight

This category is concerned with establishing the oversight mechanisms necessary to maintain an effective cybersecurity program and ensure the risk management strategy remains appropriate in the face of emerging threats.

Senior management should review the outcomes (i.e. the functions, categories, and subcategories chosen by the organization as part of its current or target profile) of the cybersecurity risk management strategy. For this to be possible, it will be necessary to develop a cybersecurity internal audit function to monitor compliance against the controls applied to achieve CSF outcomes and determine if they are effective. Such a program should examine compliance against all functions and the controls, processes, and plans that comprise them at least annually, with proportionately greater focus on the higher-risk controls (etc.).

Outcomes, and/or the methods used to achieve them, that are not contributing to the organization's goals or that have caused operational problems should be evaluated and revised.

Senior management should also review the cybersecurity risk management strategy to ensure it continues to adequately protect the organization and its assets and meet all necessary requirements. This will naturally require that contractual, operational, and regulatory requirements are checked before the review to ensure an accurate basis for comparison.

Internal (and where applicable, external) audit data can then be used to evaluate whether the strategy meets the requirements. Aggregate data can be used to develop an understanding of overall effectiveness, while sampling individual audit reports can sometimes provide deeper insight into specific issues or problems.

Finally, senior management will also be concerned with the performance of the cybersecurity program and its ongoing effectiveness. Reviewing this might involve measurements and KPIs assigned to specific controls or system components, outputs from system and network monitoring systems, audit data, and other relevant indicators that demonstrate whether controls are effective.

Where deficiencies are identified, improvements should be made. One of the biggest dangers in implementing a cybersecurity program (whether based on the CSF or any other framework) is assuming the initial implementation will always be enough to protect the organization, no matter how much the threat landscape changes.

Cybersecurity Supply Chain Risk Management

Previously part of the Identify function, this category has been moved to the Govern function and the number of subcategories increased from five to ten, reflecting an increased global focus on supply chain risk management since the publication of CSF version 1.1 in 2018.

Tackling supply chain cybersecurity can be one of the most challenging aspects of implementing a cybersecurity program. From the outset, it requires different departments to work together: HR, IT, operations, purchasing, quality, and legal all have a role to play depending on the nature of the supplier. Assigning responsibility for supply chain cybersecurity to someone who can exercise authority over all relevant departments can help the cross-departmental aspects of the program go more smoothly.

Effective supply chain cybersecurity begins with assessing the cybersecurity maturity of current and future suppliers. Many organizations begin by sending questionnaires to current suppliers, then, depending on existing contractual arrangements, progress to audits or more detailed in-person reviews if major risks are identified.

The organization will need to define roles and responsibilities related to supply chain security and to ask the same of its suppliers, particularly those that are permitted access to the organization's systems. Assessment of cybersecurity measures will also need to be built into the procurement process, with clear criteria to allow selection or rejection of potential suppliers depending on the outcome.

Cybersecurity risks associated with all suppliers should be assessed, with priority given to suppliers of critical importance or with more extensive access to the organization's systems, and mitigating measures put in place. Such measures may need to be supported by contractual changes to permit monitoring, audits, or other measures that help ensure the supplier is meeting expectations.

It is worth addressing the reality that not all suppliers will commit to cybersecurity improvements, permit in-person audits, or agree to extensive monitoring. Large-scale Cloud service providers such as Microsoft and Amazon, for example, are unlikely to allow small or medium-sized companies to conduct on-site audits at their data centers. However, they will usually provide proof of relevant independent security certifications and non-sensitive information about their cybersecurity methodologies for you to evaluate. In such 'take it or leave it' cases, it is for your organization to decide if these assurances are enough to mitigate any risks associated with use of the service. If they are not, you may be able to apply additional controls to the parts of the process you are responsible for to help balance the risk equation – or you may be forced to look for other suppliers.

Note also that the division of responsibilities in some Cloud services, such as Infrastructure as a Service (IaaS) and

Platform as a Service (PaaS), inherently requires both customer and provider to address the aspects of cybersecurity that are within their control. In such cases, it is critical that you understand where the provider's responsibilities end and yours begin. These responsibilities should be outlined in contracts or agreements to provide legal certainty.

Identify

The Identify function covers three core parts of an effective cybersecurity program: asset management, risk assessment, and continual improvement. These help you understand the data and assets you hold and the risks you face, and ensure your cybersecurity program evolves to meet future needs.

Asset Management

Effective asset management is the bedrock of your cybersecurity program. To protect assets, you first need to know what assets you hold, where they are, and how they interconnect.

The six subcategories cover developing and maintaining asset inventories for hardware, software, services, and systems (including metadata), developing and maintaining internal and external data flow maps, creating an inventory of services provided by suppliers, and prioritizing assets based on criticality and other factors.

Creating an asset inventory should be one of the first steps once the cybersecurity program is given the go-ahead, as the data you collate will underpin many other components of the program. Assets should be classified (hardware, software, information, degree of criticality, etc.) to streamline later risk assessments; where classifications overlap (and the inventory system does not support multiple categories), the more stringent category should be assigned. Many organizations opt to use dedicated software to manage their asset inventory, but a spreadsheet can also serve if resources or budget are limited.

Once the inventory is complete, you can move on to developing data flow maps that illustrate how data moves from one asset to another. As with asset inventories, dedicated software offers one route to develop these, or you could consider off-the-shelf graphing software.

Risk Assessment

Risk assessment is, naturally, at the heart of any cybersecurity program. The subcategories cover the full risk assessment process from identification through to mitigation and recording, and are broad enough to allow alignment with most common assessment methodologies, so most organizations should not have to go to great lengths to align their existing processes with the CSF.

The risk assessment drives the selection of cybersecurity controls under the Protect function, so it is essential that it is comprehensive, methodical, and based on a repeatable methodology. The data flow maps and asset inventories developed earlier, along with more technical measures such as penetration testing and automated vulnerability scanning, should be used to support the assessment and help ensure that all risks are identified and evaluated. Any risk that exceeds the tolerance threshold should be treated, whether by applying a control to reduce the risk level below the tolerance threshold, by transferring the risk to another party that can better manage it, or by terminating the activity that gives rise to the risk.

If you are unsure about the type of controls that might be applied to treat a given risk, the CSF 2.0 Reference Tool provides broad examples for a range of relevant outcomes under the Protect function that could serve as a starting point for discussion with your IT or cybersecurity team. Many of these examples are taken from NIST SP 800-53, which provides an extensive list of cybersecurity and privacy controls.

Risks are not static, and new risks arise all the time, so it is important to periodically review risk assessments. The frequency of reviews should be defined by the level of risk: Major risks should be reviewed more frequently than minor risks. A good rule of thumb is to ensure that all risks are reviewed at least once a year.

Improvement

Cybersecurity programs cannot remain static and continue to be effective, so continual improvement is essential. The four subcategories ask the organization to identify improvements from evaluations, security tests and exercises, operational processes, and incident response plans.

It is important to note that, for the most part, the evaluations, audits, tests, and associated data that improvements rely on are not explicitly incorporated into the other categories of the CSF (e.g. the Data Security category is focused on protecting the confidentiality, integrity, and availability of data and backups, but says nothing about evaluating the effectiveness of these measures to ensure the controls put in place achieve this). It will be necessary to identify both the operations, processes, and controls that require evaluation and appropriate methods of evaluation. For example, you might develop an internal audit program to validate key processes or engage an independent third party to conduct penetration testing of critical systems and networks.

There are two stages to developing an improvement program. The bulk of the work will necessarily take place toward the end of your cybersecurity program implementation project, as you need to know what the program will put in place before you can decide what to monitor and evaluate. However, while developing the program, you should consider what kind of measurement or evaluation would be appropriate for the processes and controls you are implementing – it is often easier to develop a measurement while a process is being developed than it is to come up with one after the fact (and it also allows you to modify the process to support better measurements, where necessary).

Protect

The Protect function contains a broad set of cybersecurity outcomes covering most common vulnerabilities. It has five categories, addressing identity and access control, awareness and training, and data, platform, and technology infrastructure security.

Identity Management, Authentication, and Access Control

The first step in protecting your assets and networks is to control who has access to them. Across six subcategories, the CSF asks the organization to manage identities and credentials, link identities to credentials, authenticate users, services and hardware, protect identity assertions (i.e. logins), define access permissions in a policy that applies the principles of least privilege and separation of duties, and manage physical access to assets at a level appropriate to the risk.

The principle of least privilege says that users should only be given access to the assets and information needed to perform their job, with all other access denied by default. The 'separation of duties' principle says that no user should be given sufficient privileges to allow them to misuse the system on their own. PR.AA-05 expects the organization to develop the access control policy based on these principles, and then manage, enforce, and review access permissions and authorizations on that basis.

Review frequency could be based on risk levels associated with a given category of user (e.g. administrative users reviewed more frequently than unprivileged users) but should also account for scenarios like an employee changing roles or leaving the organization.

Awareness and Training

It's easy to focus on the technological and hardware sides of cybersecurity, but people represent one of the largest vulnerabilities in any organization. This category is focused on ensuring the organization's personnel are aware of and understand their responsibilities with respect to cybersecurity.

There are only two subcategories, both with the same goal: Provide awareness and training to ensure that personnel can perform their tasks with cybersecurity in mind. One subcategory applies this requirement to personnel across the organization, while the other applies this requirement to individuals in specialized roles.

'Specialized roles' refers not only to cybersecurity personnel (who would naturally warrant more technical and in-depth cybersecurity training) but also to roles such as human resources, finance, premises security, and senior management. These roles are generally subject to greater cybersecurity risks, which the training should reflect.

Data Security

This category contains outcomes focused on protecting the confidentiality, integrity, and availability of the data the organization holds. Across four subcategories, it asks the organization to protect the confidentiality, integrity, and availability of data at rest, in transit, and in use, and to create, protect, maintain, and test backups.

The risk assessment conducted as part of the Identify function should have identified the ways data is at risk as it is used, transferred, and stored by the organization (and, where relevant, by partners and suppliers). The output of the assessment should be used to determine a set of controls that treat all risks above the organization's tolerance threshold, and it should be a relatively simple exercise to link those controls to the four subcategories. While many of the necessary controls will likely be technical, it is important not to neglect physical data security risks – for example, those related to use of portable devices or access to sensitive hard copy materials.

The subcategory on backups covers creating, maintaining, protecting, and testing of backups. Most organizations will already have backup systems in place, but these should be reviewed in light of the risk assessment, particularly in respect of protection and testing. A backup that doesn't work when you need it is no backup at all, so they should be tested regularly (this is often performed as part of incident response testing). Protection necessarily depends on the type of backup: Tapes or other physical media will need appropriate physical security measures, while digital backups usually need a combination of both (as digital backups need to be stored on hardware).

Platform Security

This category is focused on ensuring that the hardware, software, and other platforms the organization uses are managed securely.

The category addresses all platforms, whether hardware, software, or virtual, used by the organization. Its six subcategories cover configuration management, hardware and software maintenance, logging, preventing the use of unauthorized software, and using secure software development practices.

Configuration management involves defining a secure baseline state that is then applied to the software and/or devices used by the organization. A baseline configuration (sometimes called a 'gold build') might include installation of the minimum set of software programs necessary for the task, restriction of administrative tools such as PowerShell, locking down USB ports, and other controls. The organization can then deploy the baseline configuration on any new device and be confident that it is secure.

Maintaining software and hardware is a core cybersecurity practice. The organization should develop (if not already present) a policy and associated processes that ensure both automatic and manual updates are performed in a timely manner. Depending on the risks associated with the software or hardware, it may be necessary to test major updates on an isolated test system to ensure stability before rolling them out across the organization.

Secure software development may not be applicable if the organization does not develop or modify software in-house. If this subcategory does apply and the organization does not already have a secure software development methodology, NIST SP 800-218 *Secure Software Development Framework (SSDF) Version 1.1: Recommendations for Mitigating the Risk of Software Vulnerabilities* provides an excellent starting point.

Technology Infrastructure Resilience

This category is concerned with protecting networks and infrastructure against cyber and environmental threats, and with ensuring resilience and availability in both normal and adverse circumstances.

Protecting networks often requires organizations to take steps such as segmenting networks and implementing zero-trust protocols, both of which help limit the actions available to an attacker who manages to defeat or otherwise bypass perimeter controls. Organizations also often choose to restrict interaction with external elements or public networks (such as the Internet), perhaps by use of a VPN or other methods.

Protecting against environmental risks depends heavily on the nature of those risks. Systems in a flood plain require very different protective measures to those in a hurricane-prone area, for example.

Server rooms and data centers are common to many organizations, and both need adequate temperature and humidity control, cooling capacity, and monitoring systems regardless of their location. A cooling failure or similar incident could cause catastrophic damage (and perhaps even result in a major fire).

Electrical safety is another environmental risk that affects almost all organizations. Server rooms and data centers often have increased power requirements compared to normal desktop equipment, so ensuring adequate supply and performing regular maintenance checks is important. You might also consider how other safety measures, such as ceiling sprinklers, could affect the assets that network systems rely on.

Ensuring infrastructure resilience in the face of adverse events requires planning and a clear understanding of the resources necessary to ensure at least a minimum level of functionality. Uninterruptible power supplies (UPSs), redundant systems, and even backup sites can be necessary depending on the products or services you provide and the level of minimum functionality or uptime you need to maintain.

Part of this planning should involve monitoring resources such as power, cooling, and bandwidth so that you can accurately predict how much you will need during an adverse event. Resource allocations should be regularly reviewed to ensure they remain sufficient. You should also consider whether suppliers may be affected, and if so, what measures you will need to take to mitigate any impacts.

Detect

You cannot respond to a cyber attack if you do not know one is occurring. This function is dedicated to ensuring that, should an attack occur, the organization is aware and can take action. It contains two categories: Continuous Monitoring and Adverse Event Analysis.

Continuous Monitoring

Continuous monitoring means monitoring networks, hardware, and even the physical environment for events that are outside the norm (and so may indicate an attack). For most IT assets, this monitoring is often carried out by automated systems known as security information and event monitoring (SIEM) systems. These monitor network traffic, access attempts, and other relevant indicators to determine a baseline level of activity and alert IT administrators when unusual activity is detected.

At the other end of the scale, more traditional software such as antivirus and anti-malware also monitor systems for suspicious files or activity in emails, web browsers, downloaded files, and other potential threat vectors. These should be installed at every endpoint and kept up to date.

Supplier access to internal systems is increasingly common and should be monitored. This may need to be incorporated into agreements with relevant suppliers, particularly if there is a shared network boundary.

In cases where Cloud systems are used, it may not be possible to conduct your own monitoring (this depends heavily on the nature of the Cloud service), forcing you to rely on the platform provider's own monitoring systems. In such cases, you should carefully consider if the monitoring provided is sufficient and whether it is necessary.

Physical monitoring usually involves CCTV cameras positioned to cover entryways and exits or installed in secure spaces such as server rooms, manual records such as visitor logs, or electronic door locks or other mechanisms that can track the people who enter the premises.

For organizations that rent or lease their premises, or share them with other organizations, monitoring physical security involves additional challenges due to the lack of direct control over cameras and other systems. Any physical monitoring risks that the organization cannot directly address itself may need to be compensated for by additional controls elsewhere.

Where possible, monitoring should produce logs to provide an audit trail that can be reviewed should an incident occur. You might keep CCTV camera footage for three to six months, for example, while automated network monitoring systems will generate log files and reports. The output of monitoring systems – whether physical or digital – should be protected against misuse and alteration.

Adverse Event Analysis

Adverse event analysis is the process of analyzing the output of continuous monitoring systems (and any other indicators of compromise) to determine whether a given event presents a security risk. An unexpected access attempt or login from a different country, for example, could be an employee who forgot to notify IT that they would be traveling for business – or it could be the first attempt by an attacker to use compromised login credentials.

SIEM systems often perform this analysis in real time and can send alerts to mobile devices to notify users of potential security events. Some systems use machine learning and similar technologies to help differentiate between false positives and genuine security events.

Outside of dedicated SIEM systems, manual reviews of logs and other relevant outputs (CCTV footage, visitor record books, etc.) can be conducted to look for suspicious activity. Where possible, you should collate data from many different sources to help highlight trends or potentially related events.

Whether a review is conducted manually or based on a condensed report generated by a SIEM system, the people involved must have up-to-date knowledge of current threats and how they might manifest, or they risk missing potential indicators of compromise resulting from new threats. You will also need to communicate information about such events to different areas of the business and potential stakeholders – informing employees of an ongoing, targeted phishing campaign or contacting suppliers about an attack you believe may have originated from their systems, for example.

The ultimate outcome of adverse event analysis is a decision as to whether a given event or set of events constitutes a security incident. This requires clearly defined criteria against which security events can be evaluated, with those that exceed the threshold being classified as incidents.

It is sensible to provide for several levels of incident within the criteria, based on the severity of the incident in question. Large-scale data breaches involving millions of records require a different approach to a small-scale phishing attack or physical security failure, and your response will need to reflect that.

Respond

No organization is truly safe from cyber attacks, so it is essential to plan the steps the organization needs to take when the inevitable occurs. Across four categories, that is what this function is intended to achieve.

Incident Management

This category focuses on the immediate actions that follow an attack. An incident response plan appropriate to the attack should be activated, incident reports should be validated, the incident should be categorized, prioritized, and escalated to higher levels of seniority as needed, and incident recovery measures should be initiated in line with your defined criteria.

You may notice that neither development of incident recovery plans nor criteria for initiating incident recovery have been included in the preceding functions – the CSF simply assumes you have them. The expected components of such plans are (at least in part) spread across the categories in this section, so you should review the outcomes and their implementation examples carefully.

Criteria for initiating recovery refer to the various levels of incident that trigger differing responses. It is generally beneficial to have incident response plans that correspond to varying levels of compromise – a major ransomware attack, for example, requires a very different response to a local virus infection. This helps keep expenditure down and any deployed response measures appropriate to the attack in question.

If you are unsure where to start with incident response, NIST SP 800-53 (which is linked as a reference throughout this function) provides useful information on relevant controls and response measures.

Incident Analysis

This second category deals with understanding what happened (or is happening) during the attack, including finding the root cause, and recording the actions taken in response for later evaluation. You should analyze the sequence of events that began with the attack, determine which assets are affected, and identify the specific vulnerability (or vulnerabilities) that the attackers took advantage of. This helps tailor your response measures.

Relevant records, metadata, logs, and other information about your response measures should be retained and their integrity protected – precisely how should be defined in your incident response plans. This information should also be used to confirm the magnitude of the attack and identify any secondary effects.

Incident Response Reporting and Communication

The third category has only two subcategories: notify internal and external stakeholders of the incident, and share relevant information with them. Stakeholders in this context could be employees and the senior leadership team, customers, regulators, or other relevant parties. You should also consider sharing information with reputable information sharing and analysis centers (ISACs) to improve overall understanding of the attacker or attack method across the cybersecurity community.

Incident Mitigation

The final category ties in closely with your incident response plans, defining several outcomes that the organization should look to achieve to mitigate an ongoing incident. Two subcategories may not seem like much, but of all the categories, this one perhaps best exemplifies the need for multiple controls to achieve a single outcome.

The two subcategories are to contain the incident, and then to eradicate the incident. Each one contains a huge range of potential controls and are heavily dependent on the systems you operate, from something as simple as antivirus software that automatically quarantines suspicious files to advanced SIEM software that can perform a wide range of containment actions the moment an attack is detected, while simultaneously notifying key personnel to prompt further manual action.

Most organizations will need a mix of automated and manual controls when responding to an incident, and these will form the core of your incident response plans. Each plan should have clearly defined responsibilities, as confusion over authorities can cripple an otherwise effective response.

Recover

Business continuity and continual improvement play large roles in the Recover function. After responding to an incident and stabilizing the situation, it is time to fully recover. This implies returning to the status quo rather than just running on minimal functionality, in addition to taking action to prevent the incident from recurring. This recovery can happen wholesale or in stages.

The Recover function contains two categories: Incident Recovery Plan Execution and Incident Recovery Communication. Just as with incident response, the CSF does not specify the need to create a recovery plan; it assumes you have one and proceeds on that basis. If needed, NIST SP 800-53 again offers useful advice on recovery measures and controls that would be appropriate for use in such a plan.

Incident Recovery Plan Execution

Incident Recovery Plan Execution covers activating the recovery plan once the incident is contained and selecting and prioritizing recovery actions. It also asks that the organization confirm the integrity of backups and other restoration assets before using them, reestablish critical functions with cybersecurity risk management in mind, verify the integrity of restored assets and confirm the return to normal operational status, and finally call an end to the incident recovery process and complete any required post-incident documentation.

The post-incident documentation should include records and information about the actions taken during incident response and recovery, from the outset of the incident (initial detection) through to the final determination that the incident has been resolved. This documentation can then be used to perform a lessons learned analysis, helping the organization improve its response to future attacks.

Incident Recovery Communication

Incident Recovery Communication asks the organization to communicate with internal and external stakeholders about the progress of the recovery process, and to provide public communication updates (where necessary).

Senior leadership will need to be kept up to date as the recovery process progresses, and as systems and services are recovered and become available for use, relevant personnel will need to be informed. Customers will want to know that they can use your services again, and regulators may need to be updated on the successful restoration.

Developing a formal communications process helps clarify responsibilities and time frames for communication. Any public communications will need to be checked and approved before they are delivered, and internal communications benefit greatly if they are all delivered from a central source, instead of on an ad hoc basis.

CHAPTER 5: RISK MANAGEMENT

The CSF is a **risk-based** cybersecurity framework. It does not expect organizations to invest in defenses they do not need, or to have sophisticated and expensive defenses for low-level risks.

The core also respects general risk management processes, which are:

1. **Identifying risks**
2. **Determining the level of risk in terms of impact and likelihood/frequency**
3. **Comparing those risks to the organization's risk appetite (risk tolerance)**
4. **Determining an appropriate response to the level and type of risk**

Methodologies

There are several methodologies an organization can apply in assessing and managing its risks, which generally fall into two schools:

1. **Asset-based assessments**: An asset-based risk assessment examines the threats to the organization's assets and determines the vulnerabilities that those threats might exploit. A vulnerability without a threat cannot be exploited and, therefore, is not a risk. Equally, a threat with no vulnerability to exploit is not a risk.

2. **Scenario-based assessments**: Scenario-based risk assessments examine the consequences of an event more generally. For instance, what harm is likely to befall the organization if there were an earthquake? What about a break-in?

Each method has benefits and drawbacks, and the organization should consider which is most appropriate to its needs.

Risk responses

Regardless of the approach taken, the organization will need to determine how to respond to risks that exceed its risk appetite. In general terms, there are four types of response:

1. **Avoid** – terminating the source of the threat, perhaps by ending a business activity or changing the way it is done.
2. **Modify** – implementing security controls to reduce the impact and/or likelihood of the risk.
3. **Share** – transferring (part of) the risk to another party, such as through insurance.
4. **Retain** – actively choosing to tolerate the risk.

Naturally, retaining is only a good choice for very specific risks. There are typically four reasons for choosing to tolerate a risk:

1. The risk is within the organization's risk appetite – in other words, the risk is within a predefined acceptable range.

2. Mitigating the residual risk would cost too much considering its potential harm – in other words, implementing measures would be inappropriate for the level of risk.
3. It is not feasible to avoid the risk – the activity subject to the risk is essential to the organization or irreplaceable.
4. To pursue an opportunity, as some risks can have positive outcomes.

In addition, 'actual' measures – whether they consist of modifying or sharing the risk – do not have to eliminate the risk altogether. They can simply be enough to lower the risk to within acceptable boundaries. Ultimately, it is a matter of balancing the cost of treating a risk against the impact of that risk. As in many other business decisions, return on investment will remain an important principle.

In making such calculations, it is important to remember that there are often legal costs and regulatory conditions behind cybersecurity. Additionally, having strong cybersecurity measures in place may well lead to new business opportunities, which in turn result in higher revenues and a bigger customer base.

To give an example of impact considerations, would the incident make the national news, local or specialist news, or simply cause a minor discussion? If it were the latter, tolerating the reputational risk may suffice, depending on the frequency of the risk and your risk appetite. If you do take measures to reduce impact, they probably would not have to be extensive or costly. However, if the breach were likely to make the national news, more significant and costly actions may be appropriate.

There is another side to consider: Some risks can be pursued for potential positive impacts and retained on that basis. For instance, an organization may wish to move into a volatile market, which could result in significant gains or utter disaster. No matter the reason, if a decision has been made to retain a risk, this should be recorded, along with the risk owner.

Certain risk information – particularly the organization's typical cybersecurity posture and any trends – should also be passed on to stakeholders, which could include suppliers, third parties, buyers, and stockholders. For instance, it could prove useful to communicate the organization's cybersecurity risk management requirements to a potential supplier, as that supplier will need to meet those requirements too.

Ultimately, the controls that the organization selects to achieve the outcomes of each subcategory will help manage its risks. These controls should become part of the implementation plan.

NIST Risk Management Framework

The CSF naturally aligns with NIST's Risk Management Framework for Information Systems and Organizations (usually shortened to 'RMF'), which is visualized in Figure

2 below.[14] It provides a high-level view of a risk management cycle that draws on other NIST publications, including the CSF and NIST SP 800-53.

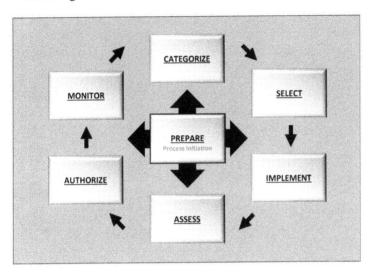

Figure 2: Visualization of the NIST Risk Management Framework

The first step is to carry out all essential tasks needed to prepare for using the RMF. Assigning key roles and responsibilities, determining a risk management strategy (including risk tolerances, etc.), identifying assets, conducting risk assessments, and other tasks are all

---

[14] NIST, NIST SP 800-37 *Risk Management Framework for Information Systems and Organizations Rev. 2*, page 9, December 2018, *https://csrc.nist.gov/projects/risk-management/about-rmf*.

necessary to provide a solid foundation on which to manage risk.

The second step involves categorizing the systems within the chosen scope, and the information that is processed, stored, and transmitted by that system. This is done based on an impact analysis, which is listed as a subcategory of the Identify function (ID.RA-04) in Appendix A of the CSF.

The third step involves the selection of a basic, initial set of security controls based on the categorization in the first step. These controls will comprise the essential controls for the organization – those it is legally or contractually required to implement, and those that enable the organization to function. Then, based on a more thorough assessment of risk and local conditions, that initial set of security controls should be expanded and tailored as appropriate – much like the categories and subcategories in the framework core.

The fourth step is to implement the selected controls. This should also be documented, along with the specifics of how those controls have been implemented.

The fifth step involves assessing the selected controls, ensuring that they have been implemented and are functioning correctly. Some controls will produce evidence that they are working as intended, for instance via logs or forms filled out by workers following a defined process, while other controls will need to be actively measured or assessed.

The sixth step is where senior management authorizes the tested and secured system. This decision is based on an assessment that looks at the residual risk. Management looks at the system as it operates, identifies how much risk is still present, and either authorizes it or decides that some sort of change is needed – whether it is more, fewer, or different controls.

The seventh step is to constantly monitor the authorized security controls and ensure that log collection, management, and analysis take place. This way, trends, unusual activities, and the control effectiveness can be identified and analyzed, and any changes can be documented and reported.

As the RMF is meant to be a continual cycle, you can then start again from step one, all the way through to step seven to account for changes in the environment or to the system itself.

For organizations looking to more closely integrate cybersecurity risk management with enterprise risk management programs, NIST SP 800-221A *Information and Communications Technology (ICT) Risk Outcomes: Integrating ICT Risk Management Programs with the Enterprise Risk Portfolio* may also be of interest.[15]

---

[15] *https://csrc.nist.gov/pubs/sp/800/221/a/final.*

CHAPTER 6: IMPLEMENTING THE FRAMEWORK

Version 2.0 of the CSF does not provide a formal implementation process, preferring instead to let the implementing organization decide how best to approach the project. However, the seven-step process provided in CSF version 1.1 remains a valid and appropriate way of implementing the framework for organizations that are not sure where to begin.

The seven-step implementation process is:

1. **Determine objectives, priorities, and scope**
2. **Identify assets and risks**
3. **Create a current profile**
4. **Conduct a risk assessment**
5. **Create a target profile**
6. **Perform a gap analysis and develop an action plan**
7. **Implement the action plan**

Step 1: Determine objectives, priorities, and scope

First, the organization identifies its business and/or mission objectives, in addition to organizational priorities – those activities and practices without which the organization would not function. After determining objectives and priorities, you can make informed decisions about the scope of the project and the organization's risk appetite.

You will also be able to start documenting the intended plan and outline of the project and assign key roles and responsibilities. As you are determining your scope, you should also provide a target time frame. Giving a lot of thought to the scoping stage is critical to avoid the project dragging on or stalling, in addition to maximizing benefits.

Step 2: Identify assets and risks

Within the determined scope, identify all your information assets and any risks and/or vulnerabilities to those assets. For example, if you were to focus on your data assets only, those assets might include:

- Records of processing activities
- Customer details
- Third-party intellectual property

When considering the potential scale of the impact in the event of an incident, reputational damage can be a significant risk factor. Other possible risk factors include personal, contractual, financial, or legal impacts – all of which could end up being costly for your organization, as they can lead to loss of revenue due to losing customers, or potentially hefty fines.

At this stage, you should decide on your overall risk methodology. This should account for your previously determined risk appetite and be informed by any regulatory or contractual requirements you may have.

Step 3: Create a current profile

The organization should develop a current profile. This should be expressed in terms of the outcomes listed in the CSF. The NIST CSF website contains templates and a quick-start guide for developing profiles; we strongly recommend these as they help clarify the process and reduce the time spent developing an in-house template.[16]

Step 4: Conduct a risk assessment

Now that the assets and their accompanying risks and/or vulnerabilities have already been identified, it is time to determine the scale of those risks and what to do about them.

Risks can be measured by combining the impact of the risk, should it materialize, with the likelihood of that risk occurring. This risk 'score' is often visualized in a likelihood/impact matrix, such as the one shown in Figure 3. Such a matrix is divided into different zones, in this case three, ranging from low-level or acceptable risks to high-level risks.

---

[16] *https://www.nist.gov/cyberframework.*

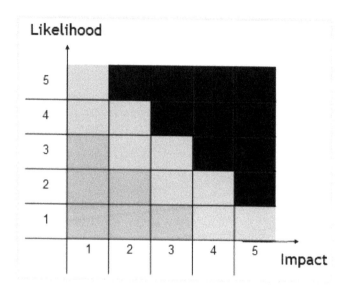

Figure 3: Example of a Likelihood/Impact Matrix

Based on these risk scores, you then decide what to do with the risks. Generally speaking, there are four options – avoid, modify, share, and retain – which were discussed earlier in this book.

Once you have determined appropriate actions for the risks you have identified, the next step is to assign priorities for implementation. The greater the risk, the higher the priority should be. You might also consider prioritizing 'quick wins' that can mitigate multiple smaller risks at once, if doing so achieves comparable impact.

Step 5: Create a target profile

The target profile should precisely define the intended outcomes of your cybersecurity project, taking everything into account that has been covered so far: objectives, priorities, requirements, identified assets and risks, and stakeholder or other external input. As with the current profile, it should be expressed in terms of the outcomes of the CSF.

Step 6: Perform a gap analysis and develop an action plan

The gap analysis compares the current and target profiles to determine the cybersecurity controls that need to be applied to achieve the outcomes in the target profile. You can use the implementation examples in the informative references spreadsheet or web interface to help select controls that are appropriate for each outcome.

The process of selecting controls should involve senior management, IT, process owners, and other relevant stakeholders from the areas of the business to which controls would be applied, as applicable to the control or outcome in question. IT support is essential when selecting technical controls, for example, while developing high-level policies will necessarily involve senior management and/or the board. Process owners likely have the clearest understanding of what happens in their area of responsibility and can point out potential pitfalls or secondary effects that might arise.

In practical terms, this is likely to be a multi-step process in all but the smallest organizations. You might begin by developing all organizational controls (policies, etc.) with support from senior management, then move on to process controls with support from process owners, then technological controls with support from IT.

As part of this process, you should also consider any measurements or monitoring necessary to ensure high-risk or critical controls work as intended. It is often easier to do this before a control has been implemented (while it is still possible to make changes) than to do so after the fact.

Throughout, you should be conscious of cost–benefit considerations and the nature of the risks each outcome is intended to address. Marked disparities in either aspect usually indicate that the selection process isn't working as it should. The CSF does not expect organizations to spend large amounts of money fixing minor risks – proportionality is key.

Once you have determined all necessary controls, you can develop an action plan to implement them. The plan should account for the priorities you assigned at the end of your risk assessment, ensuring that the most severe risks are addressed first, and any priorities that arise from the gap analysis process itself.

Step 7: Implement the action plan

Finally, you can execute the action plan. You should set clear goals, timelines, and responsibilities for each component and conduct reviews to ensure the project remains on track.

Continual improvement

These steps are intended to be repeatable, so the implemented measures are continually reviewed and improved, and the organization can progress to ever greater or more suitable levels of cybersecurity. For both the framework and cyber resilience practices more generally, it is valuable to have continual improvement processes in place. Threats and technologies change all the time, so it is essential to maintain and improve the cybersecurity measures you implement so they remain effective.

In particular, when a breach has occurred, the practices established for the Recover function should be able to both restore any assets affected and learn from the experience to improve your overall cybersecurity. However, when new requirements arise – whether these are because of a change in the industry, new regulations, or new business opportunities – the implementation model can be started again from step one – establishing a new scope – to ultimately implement a new action plan to meet your organization's new challenges.

Decision-making and implementation responsibilities

As far as the levels of decision-making and implementation are concerned, first and foremost, the executive or board deals with governance and the overall objectives and strategy, and establishes key organizational criteria, such as the risk appetite and policies.

The business or process level works within that context to develop the CSF for the organization. It defines the current and target profiles, allocates the budget, and is responsible for informing the executive level of changes in current and future risks. These changes may lead to changes in mission priorities or budget, which will have to be incorporated again into the target profile.

The implementation or operations level then implements the action plan derived from the current and target profiles. It also ensures the day-to-day functioning of cybersecurity controls runs smoothly. The operations level reports to the process level on implementation progress, and any changes in assets, vulnerabilities, or threats. These may, again, influence the target profile, resulting in further changes, and so on.

CHAPTER 7: ALIGNMENT WITH OTHER FRAMEWORKS

The CSF is an effective and flexible framework that is well-known across the United States, and increasingly across the rest of the world. However, one valid criticism of the framework is that it lacks independent verification. Even the most stringent target profile means little if the controls selected to meet outcomes are ineffective or poorly maintained.

With no independent way to verify compliance with the CSF, many organizations will ask their partners to instead achieve accredited certification to internationally recognized standards such as ISO 27001 and ISO 22301. These standards align closely with the CSF, and all three can be operated concurrently.

ISO 27001

ISO 27001 provides a specification for a best-practice information security management system (ISMS). An ISMS generally focuses on protecting the organization's information assets, and so aligns primarily with the Identify, Protect, and Detect functions, and applies processes relevant to the Respond function.

Effective cybersecurity, and therefore an effective ISMS, is founded on three 'pillars': people, processes, and technology. Ultimately, while having the right technology in place is critical to security, that technology must be managed and maintained by people, who need to follow defined processes. This is part of the systematization of information security: ensuring full coverage at any point that information could be compromised.

ISO 27001 also has a number of principles that align with the CSF's suggestions. These include:

- Governance
- Risk management
- Continual improvement

Like the CSF, ISO 27001 takes a risk-based approach to information security. It also mandates that top management takes overall responsibility for the effectiveness of the organization's information security measures, and asks that the organization determines the context it operates in to help better understand risks. This approach ensures that the ISMS is implemented in line with the organization's overall strategic direction, and helps ensure the project is more than a mere box-ticking exercise.

A key component of an ISO 27001-compliant ISMS is penetration testing – systematic and controlled probing for vulnerabilities in your applications and networks. Many cyber attacks can easily be prevented by keeping software and systems up to date. Vulnerabilities are discovered and exploited all the time by opportunistic criminal hackers, who use automated scans to identify targets. Closing these security gaps and fixing vulnerabilities as soon as they become known are essential steps to keeping your networks and information systems safe and secure.

ISO 27001's continual improvement cycle aligns with the CSF's 'Improvement' category (part of the Identify function). Both emphasize the need to continue refining and improving controls and processes to ensure the organization remains secure in the face of an ever-changing threat landscape.

ISO 22301

ISO 22301 provides a specification for a business continuity management system (BCMS). A BCMS is designed to help your organization respond effectively to disruptive events and return as quickly as possible to a minimum acceptable service level while more extensive recovery efforts are carried out – in other words, to help make your organization as resilient as possible. As such, an ISO 22301-conformant BCMS primarily aligns to the Respond and Recover functions.

As with ISO 27001, a BCMS aligned with ISO 22301 will reflect CSF core practices. They include:

- Governance
- Business impact analysis (BIA)
- Risk management
- Business continuity planning

Both ISO 27001 and ISO 22301 emphasize understanding the context in which the organization operates and management's ongoing responsibility for the overall program.

The BIA is almost certainly the most critical process involved in a BCMS. It is used to identify the organization's critical activities and their dependencies, which are in turn used to determine priorities for recovery following a disruption. The BIA will help you work out how quickly each activity needs to be resumed following an incident.

A critical outcome of the BIA is a recovery time objective (RTO) for each activity, which should also take into account that the impact of an incident usually increases with time. The RTOs will form the basis of business continuity plans (BCPs).

A BIA is not in itself enough to prepare your BCMS, however, as it only determines the value of your organization's activities. It neglects other important factors, such as:

- The specific incidents or scenarios that can affect each of these business activities
- How likely these incidents are
- How severe these incidents can be

However, a risk assessment, as previously discussed in detail, considers precisely these factors.

The content of BCPs is developed on the basis of the BIA and risk assessment, which ensures that it accurately reflects the organization's needs and specific circumstances. BCPs are the core of any BCMS, providing a plan of the actions the organization needs to take in response to any incident that threatens its key activities.

BCPs often include:

- Contact details for authorities, suppliers, and other interested parties

- Calling trees featuring key staff to ensure availability of the right competence
- Checklists or steps to be taken in the case of specific events

Ultimately, the goal is to stabilize the situation, allowing the organization to continue operating despite the incident.

It is not uncommon to find organizations that do have BCPs but not a BCMS in place. As a result, they lack the main benefits of a management system. In a full BCMS, BCPs are developed, tested, and reviewed consistently and in line with the continual improvement methodology. In addition, employees are made aware of the existence of BCPs through a formal process and understand their assigned roles and responsibilities in the event of an incident.

Combining ISO 27001, ISO 22301, and the CSF

Even when following the CSF's guidelines, it is difficult to know whether your implementation efforts are on the right track.

We believe that the best approach to cybersecurity and resilience, and maximizing your ability to survive an attack, is to implement both an ISO 27001 ISMS and an ISO 22301 BCMS and seek certification for both before implementing the CSF.

By doing so, you will have achieved many of the CSF's prescribed outcomes, which in turn will feed into current and target profiles that better demonstrate the organization's commitment to cybersecurity and remove much of the guesswork about what controls to apply to meet the CSF's objectives. You will also be able to demonstrate independently certified compliance against both standards to satisfy more demanding clients. The addition of the CSF helps cement a reputation as an organization that takes cybersecurity seriously in all the regions in which it operates, giving your customers, clients, and partners real peace of mind.

GLOSSARY

Category	Subdivisions of the framework core's functions, organizing specific cybersecurity outcomes within each function.
Control	A way of managing risk, including policies, procedures, guidelines, practices, or organizational structures, which can be of an administrative, technical, management, or legal nature.
Current profile	Description of an organization's current cybersecurity activities and their outcomes.
Cyber resilience	A system of defenses and the ability to respond to and recover from an attack when necessary.
Event	Something that occurs (or is notable by not occurring) that may or may not be an incident.

Framework core	A structured description of best-practice cybersecurity functions that protect an organization.
Framework profiles	Descriptions of how cybersecurity is handled within an organization, either currently or as a target.
Framework tiers	Descriptions of different degrees of sophistication that an organization's cybersecurity risk management might exhibit.
Function	Describes the primary subdivisions of cybersecurity outcomes within the framework core.
Incident	An event that is likely to cause harm to the organization and/or its assets.
Informative reference	References for subcategories, specifying best-practice standards, guidelines, and practices to help achieve the intended subcategory outcomes.

ISMS	Information security management system, a systematic approach to making sure confidential or sensitive information remains secure.
Risk	Several definitions are commonly used. However, one practical definition for the purposes of this book is *"the effect of uncertainty on objects."*[17]
Risk appetite	How much risk an entity is willing to tolerate.
Risk assessment	The overall process of comparing a risk against the organization's risk appetite.
Risk management	Coordinated activities to direct and control an organization with regard to risk. Typically includes risk assessment, risk treatment, risk acceptance, and risk communication.

---

[17] ISO 27000:2018, Clause 3.49.

Subcategory	Subdivisions of categories that describe specific cybersecurity outcomes.
Target profile	Description of an organization's aspirations with regard to cybersecurity risk management activities.
Threat	A potential cause of an unwanted incident, which may result in harm to a system or organization.
Vulnerability	A weakness of an asset or group of assets that can be exploited by one or more threats.

FURTHER READING

IT Governance Publishing (ITGP) is the world's leading publisher for governance and compliance. Our industry-leading pocket guides, books and training resources are written by real-world practitioners and thought leaders. They are used globally by audiences of all levels, from students to C-suite executives.

Our high-quality publications cover all IT governance, risk and compliance frameworks and are available in a range of formats. This ensures our customers can access the information they need in the way they need it.

Other books you may find useful include:

- *IT Governance – An international guide to data security and ISO 27001/ISO 27002, Eighth edition* by Alan Calder and Steve Watkins, *www.itgovernance.co.uk/shop/product/it-governance-an-international-guide-to-data-security-and-iso-27001iso-27002-eighth-edition*
- *DORA – A guide to the EU Digital Operational Resilience Act* by Andrew Pattison, *www.itgovernance.co.uk/shop/product/dora-a-guide-to-the-eu-digital-operational-resilience-act*
- *ISO 22301:2019 and Business Continuity Management* by Alan Calder, *www.itgovernance.co.uk/shop/product/iso-223012019-and-business-continuity-management-*

understand-how-to-plan-implement-and-enhance-a-business-continuity-management-system-bcms

For more information on ITGP and branded publishing services, and to view our full list of publications, please visit

www.itgovernancepublishing.co.uk.

To receive regular updates from ITGP, including information on new publications in your area(s) of interest, sign up for our newsletter at

www.itgovernancepublishing.co.uk/topic/newsletter.

Branded publishing

Through our branded publishing service, you can customise ITGP publications with your organization's branding. Find out more at

www.itgovernancepublishing.co.uk/topic/branded-publishing-services.

Related services

ITGP is part of GRC International Group, which offers a comprehensive range of complementary products and services to help organizations meet their objectives.

For a full range of cybersecurity resources, please visit *www.itgovernance.co.uk/cyber-security-solutions.*

Training services

The IT Governance training programme is built on our extensive practical experience designing and implementing management systems based on ISO standards, best practice and regulations.

Our courses help attendees develop practical skills and comply with contractual and regulatory requirements. They also support career development via recognised qualifications.

Learn more about our training courses and view the full course catalogue at

www.itgovernance.co.uk/training.

Professional services and consultancy

We are a leading global consultancy of IT governance, risk management and compliance solutions. We advise organizations around the world on their most critical issues and present cost-saving and risk-reducing solutions based on international best practice and frameworks.

We offer a wide range of delivery methods to suit all budgets, timescales and preferred project approaches.

Find out how our consultancy services can help your organization at

www.itgovernance.co.uk/consulting.

Industry news

Want to stay up to date with the latest developments and resources in the IT governance and compliance market? Subscribe to our Security Spotlight newsletter and we will send you mobile-friendly emails with fresh news and features about your preferred areas of interest, as well as unmissable offers and free resources to help you successfully   start   your   project: *www.itgovernance.co.uk/security-spotlight-newsletter.*

EU for product safety is Stephen Evans, The Mill Enterprise Hub, Stagreenan, Drogheda, Co. Louth, A92 CD3D, Ireland. (servicecentre@itgovernance.eu)

www.ingramcontent.com/pod-product-compliance
Lightning Source LLC
Chambersburg PA
CBHW041638050326
40690CB00026B/5261